DISCOVER

VAMPIRES

DO YOU BELIEVE?

This series features creatures that excite our minds. They're magic. They're myth. They're mystery. They're also not real. They live in our stories.

45TH PARALLEL PRESS

Published in the United States of America by Cherry Lake Publishing Group
Ann Arbor, Michigan
www.cherrylakepublishing.com

Reading Adviser: Beth Walker Gambro, MS Ed., Reading Consultant, Yorkville, IL
Book Design: Felicia Macheske

Photo Credits: © Casther/Shutterstock.com, cover; © Art789/Shutterstock, 1; © Lario Tus/Shutterstock, 5; © Kiselev Andrey Valerevich/Shutterstock, 7, 8, 18; © Hooked2Art/Shutterstock, 11; © Andrey Bondarets/Shutterstock, 12; © udra11/Shutterstock, 15; © Daniel Brigginshaw/Shutterstock, 17; © mountainpix/Shutterstock, 21

Graphic Elements Throughout: © denniro/Shutterstock; © Libellule/Shutterstock; © sociologas/Shutterstock; © paprika/Shutterstock; © ilolab/Shutterstock; © Bruce Rolff/Shutterstock

45th Parallel Press is an imprint of Cherry Lake Publishing.

Library of Congress Cataloging-in-Publication Data

Names: Loh-Hagan, Virginia, author.
Title: Discover vampires / Virginia Loh-Hagan.
Description: Ann Arbor, Michigan : Cherry Lake Publishing, 2023. | Series: Magic, myth, and mystery express | Audience: Grades 2-3 | Summary: "What makes a vampire weak? Do all vampires drink human blood? Books in the Magic, Myth, and Mystery Express series for young readers explore spooky creatures that go bump in the night, fill our dreams (or nightmares!), and make us afraid of the dark. Written with a high-interest level to appeal to a more mature audience and a lower level of complexity, clear visuals help struggling readers along. Considerate text includes fascinating information and wild facts to hold readers' interest and support comprehension. Includes table of contents, glossary with simplified pronunciations, and index"—Provided by publisher.
Identifiers: LCCN 2022039298 | ISBN 9781668919651 (hardcover) | ISBN 9781668920671 (paperback) | ISBN 9781668923337 (pdf) | ISBN 9781668922002 (ebook)
Subjects: LCSH: Vampires—Juvenile literature. | Animals, Mythical—Juvenile literature.
Classification: LCC GR830.V3 L64 2023 | DDC 398.21—dc23/eng/20220826
LC record available at https://lccn.loc.gov/2022039298

Cherry Lake Publishing would like to acknowledge the work of the Partnership for 21st Century Learning, a network of Battelle for Kids. Please visit *http://www.battelleforkids.org/networks/p21* for more information.

Printed in the United States of America
Corporate Graphics

Dr. Virginia Loh-Hagan is an author, university professor, former classroom teacher, and curriculum designer. She keeps vampire hours. She works at night. She sleeps during the day. She lives in San Diego with her very tall husband and very naughty dogs.

CONTENTS

CHAPTER ONE

Bloodsuckers

Vampires bite living things. Blood is their food. Vampires were once human. They're **undead**. This means they died. But they act alive. They come out at night.

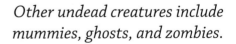

Other undead creatures include mummies, ghosts, and zombies.

Did You KNOW?

Vampires avoid children and babies. Their blood is pure. Their blood is poisonous to vampires. A dead human's blood is also bad for vampires.

There are different types of vampires. **Dhampirs** are half vampire and half human. They become **slayers**. Slayers hunt vampires.

Many vampires sleep in coffins.

Strigoi are **immortal** vampires. This means they live forever. They're evil.

Vampires sleep in dark places. They live in **covens**. Covens are vampire groups.

Most vampire stories are about strigoi.

Explained by
SCIENCE

Some people can't be in sunlight. But they're not vampires. They may have a skin condition called XP.

CHAPTER TWO

Beware of the Fangs

Vampires bite. They have strong **fangs**.
Fangs are sharp teeth. They pierce skin.

Vampire blood has a lot of iron.
It carries more oxygen.

Vampires have superpowers. They're stronger than 10 men.

Vampires are hunters. They're strong. They're smart. They don't get tired. They're sneaky.

Vampires drink blood to heal themselves.

Have You
HEARD?

Candirus live in the Amazon River in South America. They're called vampire fish. They're tiny catfish. They look for larger fish. They feed on their blood.

CHAPTER THREE

Slaying Vampires

Vampires are hard to kill. But they can be killed. Cutting off their heads kills them.

A **stake** in the heart also kills them.

Vampires can't be on holy ground.

Wooden stakes are pointy sticks. Slayers stake vampires to their coffins.

STAY SAFE!

- Make bread with vampire blood. Eat it. This way, they will not come back.

- Burn vampires. Eat the ashes. They can't be undead without their undead bodies!

Vampires hate sunlight. Sunlight burns their skin. Vampires burst into flames. They turn to ashes.

Vampires hate garlic. They have strong senses of smell.

Vampires only need to be invited inside once.

CHAPTER FOUR

Getting Bitten

Vampires bite to eat. They suck out all the person's blood. Most humans die. But sometimes, vampires don't let humans die. The humans become new vampires.

In some stories, vampires start out as "bags of blood."

Know the LINGO!

Brood: a group of vampires and their leader

Farmer: a vampire who feeds on animals, not humans

Leech: a bad word for a vampire

ORIGINS

The most famous vampire is Count Dracula. He was created by writer Bram Stoker. Count Dracula lives in Transylvania in Romania. He's based on a real person. He's based on Vlad Dracul.

A vampire kills a human. Then the human becomes undead. They have vampire blood in their bodies. They turn into vampires.

Many cultures have vampire stories.

REaL
WORLD

Maria Cristerna is called "Vampire Lady." She has a world record. She's the woman with the most body changes. She added fangs into her gums.

CONSIDER THIS!

Say What?

Read Torch Graphic Press's book *The Werewolf's Curse* by Kate Tremaine. Then reread this book about vampires. Which monster would win in a battle? Explain.

Think About It!

Vampires are everywhere. They're on television. They're in books. They're in movies. What makes vampires so interesting?

LEARN MORE

Burgan, Michael, and David Malan. *What Is the Story of Dracula?* New York: Penguin Workshop, 2020.

Largie, A. D., and Sabrina Pichardo. *Vampires Are Scary: Halloween Horror Stories for Kids*. Independent, 2017.

Glossary

covens (KUH-vuhns) vampire groups

dhampir (dahm-PEER) creature that is half vampire and half human

fangs (FANGZ) sharp teeth that suck blood from a body

immortal (ih-MOHR-tuhl) living forever

slayers (SLAY-uhrs) people, sometimes dhampirs, who hunt and kill vampires

stake (STAYK) sharp wooden stick

strigoi (STREE-goy) immortal vampires

undead (uhn-DEHD) creatures that were dead and were brought back to life

Index